Customer Resolution System

MIKE AGUGLIARO

ISBN-13: 978-1541062634
ISBN-10: 1541062639

BOOM!

Boom!

Hey, it's Mike Agugliaro, Business Warrior -- with some insight to share that's real, raw, relevant, and right now!

You've opened this report and started reading. Congratulations – this one seemingly simple step now puts you head-and-shoulders above many other business owners whose businesses are stuck in the "I-wish-it-was-different" spiral of death.

But you took the first step to get your hands on this book, and the second step to open it and read it.

Now the third step is something you may not have thought about yet – *how will you apply what you read?*

Some people will skim this report and put it on a shelf. Six months from now they'll wonder why it didn't help them.

However, I don't want to waste your time and I don't want you to waste mine, so I have a challenge for you. It's something I personally do daily and it helped to change the game for me.

Rather than reading (skimming) and putting the book away, I advise that you read actively, with a pen and highlighter in hand, and a notepad and some sticky notes nearby.

Underline and star important points; jot down notes as you go. Add sticky notes of points to revisit later. Later in this report is a TAKE ACTION section that gives you space for specific types of actions (I use a page like that whenever I read anything.)

If you've never read a book this way before, you might feel strange writing in it but I promise you: it will completely change how you read, and how much you'll benefit from what you read. (I devour books this way and the notes are beneficial to me when I re-read and review books again and again.)

I want you to enjoy a massive amount of wealth, freedom, and market domination (however you choose to define those terms in your life and business)… and actively reading this report will help you unlock more of those things for you.

What I share in this report are strategies/ideas/concepts/tools that I still use daily in my $30+ million/year business. I know these work in my business and I share them with you so you can apply them in yours too.

(These are exactly the same kinds of strategies I share in my 4-day Warrior Fast Track Academy.)

By the way, I always want to serve you at the highest level, so make sure you read all the way through to the end of the book because I have some bonus material and resources in the back that I think you'll love.

Ready? Let's dig in and get you more wealth, freedom, and market domination right now...

CUSTOMER RESOLUTION SYSTEM™

When A Customer Complains, You Can Handle It The Way You Always Have... Or You Can Follow This Strategy To Instantly Flip The Problem And Grow Your Business

As a service business owner, you know the importance and value of every single customer who calls you up and hires your company to help them.

Not only do you recognize the value of each customer, you also know how much your company invests to get in front of that customer. You built a brand, you hired a team, you invested in trucks and uniforms, and then you invested further in marketing – just to get that customer.

You did all of that to get a prospective customer to pick up the phone and call you when they needed help, which gave you the opportunity to turn them from a lead into a paying customer.

Once those customers are on your customer list, every subsequent call they make to you for service increased their value as a customer: they become more profitable because you invested once to get them in the door and now they pay you multiple times.

Acquiring new customers is critical to the ongoing operation of your business, and getting existing customers to buy from you again is critical to the increasing profitability of your business. If you want wealth, freedom, and market domination, you need to bring in new customers but just as importantly, you need to serve your existing customers again and again and again.

Critical to SUCCESS - SERVING your existing customers again & again!

The problem is, this doesn't happen very often, for two reasons:

1. Service businesses places a greater emphasis on generating new leads and doesn't actively find ways to reconnect with their existing customers.
2. Service businesses don't try to WOW customers with amazing service.

In this report, I'm going to focus on the second point (but be sure to check out my blog at CEOWARRIOR.com/blog where I talk about ways to serve your existing customers).

Put The Service Back Into Service Business

Customer service is a popular buzzword and there are plenty of so-called gurus out there who will tell you the importance of "good customer service." And if I were to informally survey most service business owners, they'd tell me proudly that they strive for achieving good customer service in their business. Perhaps you might proudly boast the same thing.

Unfortunately, good customer service is a lie that service business owners tell themselves.

Customer service is A LIE that service business owners tell themselves.

An owner might say, "Our customers love us because we give good customer service – certainly better than our competitors!" But when I press further to describe what "good customer service" means, the owner lists very standard things like, "We use the customer's name, our employees wear uniformed shirts, and we give fair written estimates," – exactly the same customer service characteristics that just about every other service business in the market does.

Customer Resolution System
By Mike Agugliaro

Service business owners think they give good customer service but all they really do is provide the barest minimum of customer service that most customers expect.

That's why I frequently say that service businesses operate at one service level lower than they think they do – so great service is actually good service, and good service is actually bad service – because they're doing what THEY think is a high level of service but it's actually just the standard that customers expect.

If you want to really stand out from the crowd and lock your business' name in the hearts and minds of your customers then you have to WOW customers with amazing service. I believe that it's possible to get your customers SO excited about your business that they call up their family and friends after your expert leaves and they say, "You won't believe the amazing service I just received …"

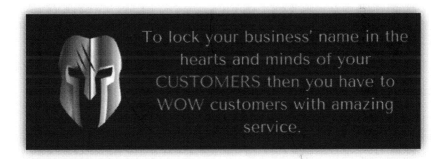

To lock your business' name in the hearts and minds of your CUSTOMERS then you have to WOW customers with amazing service.

THAT is the level of service I want my team to strive for. That's why my team does things like: call up the customer while we're on the way over and we offer to pick up some coffee for them; and when we get to their house, we'll bring up the newspaper or the empty garbage bin; and there have been times when my team has helped to bury a deceased pet and even fix a grandfather clock; and one time we had a service call cancelled because it was the customer's birthday so my team bought a cake the next day. There is so much you can do to serve your customers at a higher level and most service businesses are missing out.

When you WOW your customers, you lock your name in their minds and they call you back again when they need more service in the future.

WOW Service Is Not Just About Doing Amazing Things Proactively

I've talked about the importance of delivering amazing service, and how repeat customers are so important for your business. I need to tell you that delivering WOW service to your customers is not just about surprising them with a bunch of unexpectedly nice actions. (That's important but that's not the only thing).

Another way to separate your business from your competitors and deliver WOW service is to implement a **customer resolution system.**

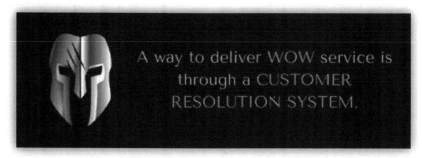

That's because you're dealing with human beings and while WOW service will help to proactively ensure that every customer is thrilled with the work they received from you, there will be times when it doesn't happen… there will be times when a customer is unhappy.

It's inevitable, even with WOW levels of service. (Fortunately, with WOW levels of service, there aren't as many). It's inevitable because we're dealing with human beings and no one is perfect. Maybe your expert was having a bad day, or made a mistake, or accidentally broke something; or maybe the customer was having a bad day, or misunderstood what the service call was for; more often than not, it's a number of little things that go wrong or are perceived incorrectly – suddenly the customer finds themselves very dissatisfied with the service they received.

What you do when a customer complaint comes in is another way to separate yourself from your competitors and stand out in your customer's mind – and having a customer resolution system in place will help to make sure that unhappy customers are addressed and often even turned around into happy customers who buy from you again.

In the first ten years of my business, when it was basically just my partner and I (and our two assistants), we worked 24/7 and nearly burned out. Our business made less than a million dollars each year and we didn't have anything in place to address unhappy customers. Any customer resolution we had to do was haphazard. Unhappy customers were dealt with on the fly, without any system or order or consistency. Some even fell through the cracks and were never dealt with at all. Imagine how THEY felt!

Then, after nearly burning out, my business partner and I committed to making changes in our business, to start working on the business (instead of in the business) and doing whatever we could to turn the business around and grow it strategically. The transformation we made was amazing and ten years after that shift, we've grown every single year and are on track this year to make $32 million. We've had an amazing second decade of business since that transformation.

One of the things we put in place was a customer resolution system – a strategic, consistent way to work with customers who were not happy. And this customer resolution system is what I want to share with you in this report.

Unhappy Customers Are An Opportunity

Most service business owners fear unhappy customers. They worry about getting negative complaints (especially negative complaints that are posted online for everyone to see). Unhappy customers tell their friends about their negative experience. But many of these service business owners are the same ones who are only giving "good customer service" (which you'll recall is one level lower – so it's really bad customer service!)

Service business owners who strive for WOW levels of service see UNHAPPY CUSTOMERS as an OPPORTUNITY.

However, not all service business owners fear unhappy customers! Service business owners who strive for WOW levels of service see unhappy customers as an opportunity.

- They're an opportunity to turn an unhappy customer into a happy customer – yes, even one who will call your company back again in the future.
- They're an opportunity to identify gaps or shortfalls in your business that need to be addressed to ensure you're delivering WOW levels of service to everyone.
- They're an opportunity to stretch yourself and see how you can creatively provide WOW service even when there's adversity.
- They're an opportunity to build new WOW service into your business so that a similar complaint never happens again.

You should be glad when unhappy customers contact you. Of course you shouldn't be glad that you have an unhappy customer but you should be glad that they contacted you because it gives you a chance to make it right and to make your business stronger.

That's why I'm providing you with the exact customer resolution system that I implemented in my business more than a decade ago when my business partner and I made our game-changing transformation for growth. We've tweaked this system over the years to perfect it, and we still use it today in the business. This customer resolution system is responsible for millions of dollars in revenue because every time we used it, we became a better, stronger company that served every subsequent customer at a higher level.

I'm sharing it with you so you can implement it into your business and become a better, strong company. What's more, you can implement it now and shave years off of the learning curve that I had to go through to learn its importance!

How To Use The Customer Resolution System

Print the Customer Resolution System on the next page and share it with everyone in your office. Make sure everyone has copies of it – especially those who deal with the public. However, I recommend that everyone in your company has at least a passing familiarity with it because you never know when a customer might call, or who a customer might call.

Customer Resolution System
By Mike Agugliaro

Most importantly, your customer service reps or phone support staff should be very familiar and comfortable with it, as should your managers – so that the issue can be escalated if necessary. And when I say "they should be familiar with it," I mean that your frontline team should fill out several of them as practice so that they aren't just reading the sheet for the first time while talking to an unhappy customer.

When a customer calls, go through the sheet and answer as many questions as are appropriate. (Some questions don't need to be answered on the call, and some questions the customer won't know the answer to.) Be polite; use empathy; express concern and understanding; ask the questions without interrogating; deal with their concerns quickly and efficiently.

Be polite; use empathy; express concern and understanding; DEAL WITH THEIR CONCERNS QUICKLY and efficiently.

This sheet isn't just a "fill-out-the-answers" sheet – **think of it as a work order for the customer's satisfaction. Their happiness with your business is broken and this is the work order to fix it!**

Your target for filling this out is NOT to compensate the customer so they won't post an angry message about you online. Rather, your target for filling this out is the same as it was when you went to their house the first time – **to shock them with your WOW level of service and the lengths that you'll go to make sure they're amazed.**

And as the owner, these are one of the most important things you and your executive team should be looking at regularly. Every month, grab the last 30 days of complaints and look through them (or even go back further to the last 90 days). Look for patterns or people or situations that happen again and again. You'll make better decisions and have a clearer view of your business from this regular practice.

Summary

Every service business succeeds at a higher level when more of their happy customers call back for more service and tell friends about the amazing service they received. You should strive to deliver WOW service every time. But even if you do, you won't please everyone 100% because we're imperfect and we deal with imperfect human beings. Fortunately, when an unhappy customer calls you, that's a good thing because it's an opportunity for you to become stronger from the adversity and to rise above the situation to become a better company as a result.

This Customer Resolution System is a simple one-page document but it is VERY powerful when you become familiar with it and when you deploy it in your business to help you become more successful. This document is responsible for millions of dollars in my business because every time we filled it out, we learned from it and became a better company. Do the same in your business and you'll never fear an unhappy customer again.

Permissions: *The Customer Resolution System, pictured on the next page, can be photocopied from this book and used in your own company. You can also create your own version and adjust if necessary.*

Customer Resolution System
By Mike Agugliaro

	Tech	
Date of Call		
Date Resolution		
	OFFICE USE ONLY	

CUSTOMER RESOLUTION FORM

We Do More!

Nature of the complaint:

	PRICE:		VALUE:		DAMAGE	
Name:		Home Ph.		Cell Ph.		
Address:		City, State:			Zip:	
Job #:	Inv #			Date of work:		
Payment Method:			Tech:		CSR:	
Date call taken:		Who is calling w/ complaint:				

	Questions to ask the customer	Yes	No
1.	Did our expert review the problem with you?		
2.	Did our expert give you options to choose from?		
3.	Did our expert quote you an exact price prior to doing the work?		
4.	Did our expert have you sign the work order to approve the work prior to starting?		
5.	Did you sign the work order where it stated you were 100% satisfied with the work performed?		

What would make a customer a raving fan:

Action Taken:

What would make a customer a raving fan:

Action Taken:

Credit Amount: _____   Refund Amount: _____   Check / CC: _____

Comments and Recommendations From Service Center T/L	**Comments**

Date tech briefed:	SVC MGR.	Owner / Director:

Recommended future action:

Wait! You're not done yet. If you put this report on the shelf now, you'll risk completely wasting the strategies and ideas you just read. Turn them into action right away. On the next page you can start turning my ideas into your business-building action. Fill it out right now...

TAKE ACTION

Want to extract all the value you can from this report? Don't just put this book on the shelf. Review this report and fill out the list below, writing out the actions you should stop doing, keep doing, and start doing. On the next page is space to make additional notes. And for further actions, be sure to continue reading the bonus report and added strategies and resources on the following pages!

Stop Doing (Actions you're doing now but need to stop doing)

\
\
\
\

Keep Doing (Actions you're doing now and should continue)

\
\
\
\

Start Doing (Actions you're not doing now but should start)

\
\
\
\

Additional Notes

_____

_____

_____

_____

_____

_____

_____

_____

_____

_____

_____

_____

_____

_____

_____

_____

_____

_____

_____

_____

_____

_____

SPECIAL REPORT:
NETWORKING YOUR WAY TO BROKE

HERE'S HOW SERVICE BUSINESS OWNERS FIND THE ONE
INDUSTRY GROUP THAT WILL ACTUALLY MAKE A
MEASURABLE DIFFERENCE TO THEIR BUSINESS' GROWTH…
INSTEAD OF THROWING MONEY AWAY AT HIGH-COST,
LOW-VALUE MEMBERSHIPS

This report is for service business owners – including plumbers, HVAC, and electricians – who understand the importance that an industry organization or group can play in the growth of their business.

If you are either currently looking for an industry organization or group to join or are disappointed by the results you're (not) getting from the organization you currently belong to, then make sure you read this report all the way through because you may be surprised by what you learn…

You're on a journey and you reach a fork in the road. But not just two potential paths… Rather, you have a dozen or more potential paths. Each path promises to help you get to your preferred destination but when you look at the dejected faces of people traveling in the opposite direction, you know that not every path will do what it promises.

Welcome to the world of home service industry organizations and groups. There are many available and each one promises to train you to grow your service business with the latest strategies and industry best practices, to provide networking opportunities, and perhaps discounts on marketing or services.

Unfortunately, many service business owners learn the hard way that these organizations are not delivering on their promise; instead, they

happily accept your hard-earned money for their expensive memberships but rarely deliver back the value you hope to get.

Year after year you promise yourself, this year I'll dig deeper to get more out of the group, or, this year I'll try a different group; but you get to the end of every year and discover that nothing has changed. Your money has been wasted. (And yet, if you're like most service business owners, you continue in the organization because you hope that next year will bring you the value you need.")

The results speak for themselves: you might take away a half-decent idea now and then, or you might benefit from the occasional group call… but you have a hard time justifying the membership cost.

Forget the empty promises of training and networking that will once again fall through.

What do service business owners really want? If you're like most service business owners out there, you probably want **practical ideas that you can implement immediately to get fast results; and, to be frank, you might even benefit from the occasional get-your-ass-in-gear push to help you overcome the frustrations and obstacles that plague you daily.**

Use this list to diagnose whether you're wasting your money at your current industry organization or group, and to see what option will actually create positive measurable growth in your business.

#1. Are The Owners "In The Trenches" Every Day?

Some industry organizations and groups are run by people who haven't run a home service business in years; others are run by people who have never worked a single day in the home service industry!

CEO Warrior is owned by Mike Agugliaro and Rob Zadotti, who also own Gold Medal Service. Gold Medal Service is New Jersey's #1 home service business, employing 190 staff, serving 125,000 customers, and will earn more than $30 million this year. Mike and Rob still run their home service business and are always learning and testing to share only the strategies that have proven to work.

Would you rather hear from someone who is no longer in the business or someone who is still in the business daily?

#2. Have The Owners Of Your Industry Organization Discovered The Path To Success?

Many industry organizations simply pass down their best practices from one generation to the next, and those who run the organization just "parrot" what they've heard before. If they're in the industry, they're just moderately successful… or perhaps have merely inherited their thriving home service business rather than built it up from scratch.

Mike and Rob started out as electricians. For the first decade of their business the two of them worked 24/7 and struggled to make ends meet. After nearly burning out and shutting the business down they decided to fix what was broken, so they invested heavily in their own education then rebuilt the business from the ground up. The next eleven years were completely different, with year-over-year growth of more than a million dollars annually.

Would you rather get "hearsay advice" that is parroted from a previously successful person, or learn the strategies and systems from the same person who struggled then figured it out?

#3. Do the Owners Invest Heavily In Education?

If you currently belong to an industry organization or group, find out what the owners have learned recently. Ask them. Do they have a growing knowledgebase of current field-tested strategies that they've culled from the best-of-the-best?

CEO Warrior does! Mike and Rob have invested more than $900,000 into their education and have studied the best strategies even from organizations outside of the home service industry. Disney, Zappos, Amazon,

Nordstrom, Joe Polish, and others — CEO Warrior mines the best strategies from these best-of-the-best companies.

Do you prefer stale strategies that have not been updated in years or the latest field-tested ideas inspired by the world's best-of-breed companies?

#4. Does The Industry Organization Have A Million Dollar Guarantee?

When you attend an industry event, what kind of guarantee do they have? Many don't offer any kind of guarantee; at best, you might hear the vague "If you're not satisfied, we'll try to make it right" promise.

CEO Warrior's 4-day Warrior Fast Track Academy events come with an iron-clad $1 million dollar guarantee that promises: **"If you get to the end of the very first day and you haven't learned enough strategies that will make you an extra million dollars or save you a million dollars, then simply ask for a refund and you'll get 100% of your tuition, PLUS the cost of airfare and hotel to get to the event, on the spot... no questions asked."**

What's the guarantee of the industry event you attend?

#5. Does The Industry Organization Provide Swipe-And-Deploy Marketing Templates?

Many home service business owners fiercely protect their marketing and will never share it. That same thinking is carried over into industry organizations where you might (but probably won't) get "plain vanilla" marketing ideas that may or may not work.

CEO Warrior is different, though. You get a binder that is literally stuffed with marketing templates that are actually being used right now in the marketplace, bringing in millions of dollars of business monthly for Gold Medal Service. When you receive these marketing templates at a 4-day Warrior Fast Track Academy event, you have permission to modify and use them in your own business – and you'll even be introduced to the name of the printer who can print them for you!

In your current industry group, were you handed a big swipe file and introduced to the exact people who were able to deploy it for you?

#6. Does The Industry Organization Feel Like A Brotherhood?

When you attend an industry event at your organization, what does it feel like? Do you nod silently to the other attendees before stealing a quick glance at their name tag because you can't remember who they are? You barely remember anyone's names because you just don't engage with these people enough.

At CEO Warrior, you may join the CEO Warrior Circle, which is a tight-knit brotherhood of service business owners. You'll be on a first-name basis and think of these other men and women as more than just colleagues – but as friends, family, and fellow "Warriors" as you fight together to grow your service businesses. CEO Warrior Circle members become a family and will do ANYTHING for each other, supporting each other professionally and personally.

When was the last time you felt like you were part of a close-knit brotherhood that cared about your success?

#7. Are You Just Paying For Friendships?

In most organizations, you're paying that expensive membership fee for what – a few friendships that you might or might not value outside of the networking event?

At CEO Warrior, you'll make solid friendships with other CEO Warrior Circle members but the real value of the group is the life-changing results that can transform your business and deliver more wealth, freedom, and market domination. You'll be connected to a strong group of fellow Warriors, each of whom is highly interested in your success. You'll make friends, yes, but you'll discover that the CEO Warrior Circle is all about helping you grow your business to create the business and life that you want.

Wouldn't you rather invest in yourself and your business than for expensive friendships?

#8. Do The Large Companies Just Promote Themselves?

In many industry organizations and groups, you'll encounter business owners of all sizes... And usually the small guys will chase around the big guys and try to find out what their secrets are (only to have the big guys simply promote themselves without ever sharing good ideas.)

CEO Warrior Circle is not about self-promotion but about everyone pulling together so that everyone can win. Each Warrior steps up and is willing to help the others. **What kind of brotherhood is CEO Warrior Circle? You could probably call any of them in the middle of the night for an emergency and they'd be there for you. Could you do that in your current industry organization or group?**

Would you rather hear a big company talk about themselves or a successful company share their best ideas with you?

#9. How Long Do You Have To Wait To Get Support?

One frustration that you may have with your industry organization is how long you have to wait to hear back from someone, especially if you're looking for help or advice. Maybe they only respond during business hours, or maybe they promise a 48 hour window to reply.

Mike and the CEO Warrior team are very responsive – **offering insight and advice in social posts, live video, email, and text messages at just about any time of day or night.** They recognize how important the Warriors are and they strive to serve them.

Would you rather wait hours (or days) to get help, or get help right away?

#10. Does Your Organization Take A One-Size-Fits-All Approach?

Nothing is more frustrating than getting some useful-sounding strategies… only to discover that these strategies only work in a business that is different than yours. Maybe you run a rural business but the ideas only work in town; maybe you have a team of 5 but the ideas only work if you have a team of 100.

CEO Warrior serves businesses of all sizes, in all locations. No matter how your business is configured, the strategies and guidance you'll receive will be custom-tailored to fit YOUR unique situation. There are Warriors all over the world – every size of business in many different markets. The strategies you get will work in your situation. Period.

Would you rather hear general advice that might not apply to you or the best field-tested strategies that will work in your specific situation?

#11. Is There An Emphasis On Growing Your Business Or Growing Your Life?

The last time you were at an organization or group event, how much emphasis was placed on your life? Probably very little. Most industry organizations try to help you grow your business – that's their purpose. Problem is, they don't care where you get the time and energy to make the necessary changes.

At CEO Warrior, the emphasis is on growing your business so that you can have the life you want. You'll learn the strategies to grow your business and you'll also discover how a healthy family life can help your business (and vice versa). You'll even hear how to stay healthy through the life and lifestyle of a service business owner.

Why grow your business at the expense of your family when you can have both – a successful business and a fulfilling family life?

#12. Does Your Group Tell You The Honest Truth, Even If It Hurts?

Most of us want to hear nice things – but if you're reading this then you're smart enough to know that a hurtful truth is better than a comforting lie. Yet, how often does your industry organization or group say something harsh but necessary? (Hint: they probably won't because they want you to renew your membership!)

Mike Agugliaro is known for his no holds barred, no BS approach. If a Warrior needs to hear something, Mike will say it. The honest truth, even if occasionally hurtful, is far more advantageous to hear. And, it's not just an honest truth told to you, there's also ongoing accountability to "hold your feet to the fire" to help you do what you say you're going to do.

If you'd rather be lied to, then join some other group. But wouldn't you rather hear the truth if it benefits you?

#13. Does Your Group "Nickel-And-Dime" You For Different Services?

In a lot of industry groups and organizations, members pay a membership fee to get access to a few things, and then they're expected to pay extra for additional products and services (like events and extra coaching).

CEO Warrior Circle members enjoy an all-inclusive experience where unlimited coaching, events, and resources are included as part of the membership investment. You simply won't get another bill for needing extra help.

Does your current group or organization care more about the fee or about you?

#14. Do You Get To Learn Directly From The Guru, Or Are You Pushed Off To Some Trainer-For-Hire?

Maybe this has happened to you: you pay your membership fee and you look forward to hearing from the guru or main person behind the group... until you actually start to interact with the group and you find out that you're stuck with a trainer-for-hire working out of a call center who follows a script and references the same resources you received when you first joined.

CEO Warrior Circle members get full access to Mike and Rob and the Master Coach Trainers – an elite group of experts who are in the industry daily. Whether by phone, text, or email (as well as webinars and events), you'll interact with the same gurus who start CEO Warrior Circle.

When was the last time you heard from the guru in your group?

#15. Do You Learn Cutting Edge Internet Marketing Strategies?

A lot of groups teach generic marketing strategies with little, if any, internet marketing. And many groups that do teach internet marketing are teaching things that worked for them 5, 10, and even 15 years ago.

CEO Warrior Circle members get the latest cutting edge internet marketing strategies that work right now for service businesses – and the reason these work is because they're being constantly tested and refined.

How current are the internet strategies you've learned? (Have you learned any? Are they currently being used?)

#16. Do They Share A Lot Of Information For Free?

Most industry groups will make a lot of promises about what you'll get when you join and force you to pay thousands of dollars to actually access the information. Very few will even give you a little glimpse into what you can learn, forcing you to put up a lot of money to find see if they're for real.

At CEO Warrior, you can learn so many strategies – whether by books, social media (Facebook, LinkedIn, and Twitter), or CEOWARRIOR.com, Mike shares many of his best ideas and strategies. In fact, one person watched Mike's free videos and applies his strategies over a 2-year period and increased the number of techs in his business from six to 20. And, many more business owners see even bigger results faster by attending Mike's 4-day Warrior Fast Track Academy

Could you more-than-triple your workforce from the free information provided by your industry group?

#17. Do You Get A Free 30 Minute Strategy Session To Even See If This Is The Right Fit For You?

Most industry organizations and groups will tell you to pay if you want to find out whether it's right for you or not. You risk your money and time without really knowing until it's too late whether the information you're learn is helpful. Perhaps they throw some generic ideas at you in an attempt to wow you but they're just regurgitating the same information for everyone.

At CEO Warrior, no one can attend the Warrior Fast Track Academy without first getting a free 30 minute strategy session with Mike, Rob, or a Master Coach Trainer. These strategy sessions are FOR you and ABOUT the strategy, problem, question, challenge, or opportunity of YOUR choosing. Simply share the struggle you want help with and the Master Coach Trainer will work with you – for free – before you can even attend the Warrior Fast Track Academy.

When was the last time you got a 30 minute free personal one-on-one strategy session with your industry organization before they even allowed you to move forward with them?

#18. Are There Events That Your Family Wants To Attend (That Actually Help Your Family Members Understand What You Do?)

Most industry events are technical and boring. Your family begs not to go, and they don't really care what you learn while you're there. But wouldn't it be nice if they could attend to understand what you do? And wouldn't it be amazing if they had such a good time that they begged to go back again? CEO Warrior Circle members often bring their spouses to events – from regular Circle events to special Warrior Relationship events, your spouse will love the event and will have a better understanding of what you do so they can support you as you grow your business.

When was the last time you attended an event with your spouse… and your spouse asked to go back again?

#19. Do You Dread Those BORING Live Events?

Most industry events are a bore! Look around the room and you'll see people trying to stay awake while the speaker drones on and on. You keep checking your watch. You drain your coffee cup and can't wait for a break to refill it. You spend more time checking your phone for messages than you do watching another boring PowerPoint slide presentation.

CEO Warrior events, including the Warrior Fast Track Academy, are anything but boring. Audiences are captivated by Mike's style, by his strategies, and by his level of service that he brings to every presentation. Some CEO Warrior Circle events even include firewalking! Make sure you get a good night's sleep before the event because you'll be "on" the entire time, and you'll leave with a level of inspiration and energy you didn't think was possible!

When was the last time you actually were excited about attending an industry event?

#20. Do You Leave The Live Event With A Road Map Of Success?

Many people attend industry events with the hope of getting a couple of good ideas that they can bring back to their company (and sometimes they'll even remember to implement those ideas when they get back!)

But those who attend Mike Agugliaro's Warrior Fast Track Academy events get something different: you'll work WITH Mike throughout the 4-day event to create your own customized 90 Day Road Map that outlines the step-by-step strategies you want to implement in your business to grow in the next 90 days. And by the end of the event, Mike and his team will even check your Road Map to make sure it's clear and achievable so you can start implementing it immediately. (Some attendees even start implementing before they leave the event.)

When was the last time you left an industry event with a multi-million dollar step-by-step Road Map to implement in the next 90 days?

The choice is yours – will you continue paying for an industry group or organization that…

… doesn't deliver what it promises?
… takes your money and then asks for more?
… feels like an expensive way to meet a few other friends in the industry?
… is difficult to reach anybody when you need real help?
… doesn't share the best, most effective field-tested strategies and ideas?
… run by people who aren't in the industry?
… doesn't seem to care about your business (or your family)?

Or, will you finally step and realize that YOU and YOUR BUSINESS (and YOUR FAMILY) are worth making the switch to a group like CEO Warrior – a true brotherhood of like-minded business owners who want help each other, led by an industry leader who will always be there for you?

The very first step to learn more about how CEO Warrior is different is to attend the 4-day Warrior Fast Track Academy – to learn more, to get many of the benefits described above, and to see if the CEO Warrior Circle is right for you.

Go to <u>WarriorFastTrackAcademy.com</u> to apply.

Are you tired of treading water – staying busy in your business but never really getting ahead? **Are you ready to discover the most powerful strategies to create real change, growth, and market domination in your business?**

Whether you're new and totally overwhelmed or you're a seasoned pro and looking for to reignite, The **Warrior Fast Track Academy** can show you how to get to the next level.

Warrior Fast Track Academy is my 4-day hands-on event where I guide you and a group of like-minded service business owners through the exact plan that I used to build a $30+ million (and growing) business. I'll reveal the blueprint and show you how you can implement the same blueprint into your business, with all areas of mastery planned out and ready to be plugged in. You'll be motivated and inspired to lead positive, profitable change in your company and take your business to never-before-seen heights.

Business owners who have attended the Warrior Fast Track Academy have said it's "life changing" and gone on to build successful businesses all around the world.

If you want to take control of your business and your future, Warrior Fast Track Academy is THE event to make that happen. To see what others are saying about Warrior Fast Track Academy, to learn more about my $1 million guarantee, and to pre-register for an upcoming event, go to WarriorFastTrackAcademy.com

"You are the average of the 5 people you spend the most time with."
(Jim Rohn)

... Who are YOU spending time with?

Here's the fastest way to leverage the power of proximity by spending time with like-minded action-takers who work together – to grow your business while striving to become unstoppable.

Most industry groups and organizations take your money and give you just a few stale best practices and networking opportunities. But at CEO Warrior, we've created **a powerful, exclusive "family of Warriors" who discover the best secrets and field-tested strategies, and who hold each other accountable while implementing them.**

Welcome to the **exclusive, invitation-only CEO Warrior Circle** where business owners can join to become Warriors and inspiring leaders of a strong and growing business.

During the upcoming year, we'll revolutionize your business and your life. We'll blow your wealth, freedom and personal goals out of the water by focusing on massive business building and life strategies. From weekly calls to exclusive events, from one-on-one coaching to an exclusive vault of swipe-and-deploy resources, joining the CEO Warrior Circle gives you everything you need to grow your business.

This program is designed for action-takers who are ready to make the commitment and take action to boost their business.

To learn more about the Warrior Circle, and to see if you qualify to participate in the Mastermind, get in touch at CEOWARRIOR.com/contact

READ THE FREE MAGAZINE WRITTEN FOR THE HOME SERVICE INDUSTRY

Discover new information, insight, and industry-specific success stories in Home ServiceMAX – the free online magazine written for home service business owners.

Each issue of Home ServiceMAX is packed with practical tips and strategies that you can implement right away into your home service business. They're field-tested and written by experts and industry insiders.

Home ServiceMAX will help you improve your sales, marketing, finance, human resources and customer service. Keep it on hand as you develop best practices to meet your team's unique challenges.

Whether you're a plumber, electrician, carpenter, roofer, builder, painter or specialist in any other service industry trade, to survive you must also stand out as a business leader. We designed this magazine to help you achieve that goal.

Each easy-to-read issue is available online for free. Check out the articles and make sure you have a pen and paper in hand to write down all the actions you'll want to take when you're done each article.

Read the current issue and subscribe here: HomeServiceMaxMag.com

ABOUT THE AUTHOR

Mike Agugliaro, Business Warrior

Mike Agugliaro helps his clients grow their service businesses utilizing his $30 Million Warrior Fast Track Academy Blueprint, which teaches them how to achieve massive wealth and market domination.

Two decades ago he founded Gold Medal Electric with his business partner Rob. After nearly burning out, he and Rob made a change: they developed a powerful blueprint that grew the company. Today, Gold Medal Service is now the top service industry provider in Central New Jersey. With over 190 staff and 140+ trucks on the road, Gold Medal Service now earns over $30 million in revenue each year.

Mike is a transformer who helps service business owners and other entrepreneurs master themselves and their businesses, take control of their dreams and choices, and accelerate their life and business growth to new heights. Mike is the author of the popular book The Secrets Of Business Mastery, in which he reveals 12 areas that all service business owners need to master.

Mike speaks and transforms around the world; his Warrior Fast Track Academy events are popular, transformational events for service business owners; he also leads a mastermind of business owners known as Warrior Circle. Mike has been featured in MSNBC, Financial Times, MoneyShow, CEO World, and more.

Mike is an avid martial artist who has studied karate, weaponry, jujitsu, and has even developed his own martial art and teaches it to others. The discipline of martial arts equips him to see and act on opportunities, create change in himself and others, and see that change through to successful completion.

Mike is a licensed electrician and electrical inspector, he is a certified Master Fire Walk Instructor, certified professional speaker, and a licensed practitioner of Neuro-Linguistic Programming (NLP).

Whether firewalking, breaking arrows on his neck, studying martial arts, transforming businesses, or running his own business, Mike Agugliaro leads by powerful example and is changing the lives and businesses of service business owners everywhere.

Mike lives in New Jersey with his wife and two children.

IN THE MEDIA

An article published in the HVACR Business Magazine discussing the struggles of being a service business owner and sharing his Situation Analysis Tool to help make better business decisions.

READ

ceowarrior.com/hvacr

Featured in a TV segment on the Nightly Business Report on CNBC. This interview shares how Mike, as an electrician, started his own business and is now advising other entrepreneurs how to be a CEO Warrior in their business.

WATCH

ceowarrior.com/cnbc

This article is about strategies to build a strong and productive team. This is one of many articles that Mike has published through Comfortech.

READ

ceowarrior.com/contractor

CEOWORLD MAGAZINE

Mike shares 5 powerful mindset shifts to rapidly grow your business. These are some that helped him grow his $28M business.

READ

ceowarrior.com/ceoworld

IN THE MEDIA

Mike shares tips on how to motivate your staff by discovering their why. It's a strategy he uses to leverage and motivate his staff of 190 with great success.

READ

ceowarrior.com/thenews

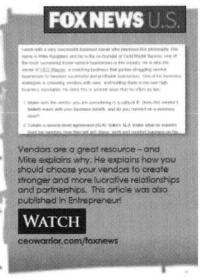

Vendors are a great resource – and Mike explains why. He explains how you should choose your vendors to create stronger and more lucrative relationships and partnerships. This article was also published in Entrepreneur!

WATCH

ceowarrior.com/foxnews

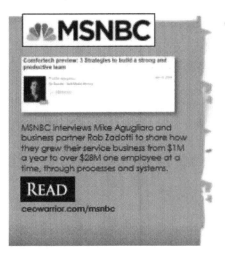

MSNBC interviews Mike Agugliaro and business partner Rob Zadotti to share how they grew their service business from $1M a year to over $28M one employee at a time, through processes and systems.

READ

ceowarrior.com/msnbc

CBS8 featured an article about Mike, CEO Warrior and the 4 Day Warrior Fast Track Academy and how it helps service business owners.

READ

ceowarrior.com/cbs8

The Secrets Of Business Mastery: Build Wealth, Freedom and Market Domination For Your Service Business in 12 Months or Less. A chapter-by-chapter collection of best business practices, tools and strategies for service business owners.

Secrets of Leadership Mastery: 22 Powerful Keys To Unlock Your Team's Potential and Get Better Results: 22 powerful keys to help you create a culture where you build and lead a hardworking team of superstars, inspire them to give their very best, and generate measurable results.

Secrets of Communication Mastery: 18 Laser Focused Tactics To Communicate More Effectively. We all communicate. We can all learn to communicate more effectively. When you do, you'll see instant results in every personal and professional relationship.

Timeless Secrets of A Warrior. Discover the most powerful, time-tested Warrior secrets that will propel you toward success by revealing strategies from some of history's greatest minds.

9 Pillars Of Business Mastery Program: Discover the nine most powerful and transformative strategies that are PROVEN to completely transform your business and your life.

CONNECT WITH MIKE AGUGLIARO

Connect with Mike in the following places and find even more free resources and strategies to help you grow your business.

Website: CEOWARRIOR.com – Go here now to get free resources, including chapters from Mike's book and a library of resources.

Warrior App: CEOWARRIOR.com/warriorapp – stay up-to-date on the latest strategies and events by downloading the Warrior App for iOS and Android.

Podcast: CEOWARRIOR.com/podcast

Events: CEOWARRIOR.com/events

Social: Visit CEOWARRIOR.com to connect with Mike on Facebook, Twitter, LinkedIn, and elsewhere.

Home ServiceMAX Magazine: HomeServiceMaxMag.com

Made in the USA
Middletown, DE
14 August 2017